100 SOLO FLUTE

Arranged by Robin De Smet.

D1650049

WISE PUBLICATIONS
LONDON/NEW YORK/PARIS/SYDNEY/COPENHAGEN/MADRID

EXCLUSIVE DISTRIBUTORS:
MUSIC SALES LIMITED
8/9 FRITH STREET, LONDON W1V 5TZ, ENGLAND.
MUSIC SALES PTY LIMITED
120 ROTHSCHILD AVENUE, ROSEBERY, NSW 2018, AUSTRALIA.

BOOK DESIGN BY PEARCE MARCHBANK STUDIO

THIS BOOK © COPYRIGHT 1984, 1994 BY
WISE PUBLICATIONS
ORDER NO. AM38365
ISBN 0-7119-0601-7

YOUR GUARANTEE OF QUALITY
AS PUBLISHERS, WE STRIVE TO PRODUCE EVERY BOOK TO THE HIGHEST COMMERCIAL STANDARDS.
THE BOOK HAS BEEN CAREFULLY DESIGNED TO MINIMISE AWKWARD PAGE TURNS
AND TO MAKE PLAYING FROM IT A REAL PLEASURE.
THROUGHOUT, THE PRINTING AND BINDING HAVE BEEN PLANNED TO ENSURE A STURDY,
ATTRACTIVE PUBLICATION WHICH SHOULD GIVE YEARS OF ENJOYMENT.
IF YOUR COPY FAILS TO MEET OUR HIGH STANDARDS, PLEASE INFORM US AND WE WILL GLADLY REPLACE IT.

MUSIC SALES' COMPLETE CATALOGUE DESCRIBES THOUSANDS OF TITLES AND IS
AVAILABLE IN FULL COLOUR SECTIONS BY SUBJECT, DIRECT FROM MUSIC SALES LIMITED.
PLEASE STATE YOUR AREAS OF INTEREST AND SEND A CHEQUE/POSTAL ORDER FOR £1.50 FOR POSTAGE TO:
MUSIC SALES LIMITED, NEWMARKET ROAD, BURY ST. EDMUNDS, SUFFOLK IP33 3YB.

Annie's Song.

Words and Music by John Denver.

Moderately

Sing.

Words and Music by Joe Raposo.

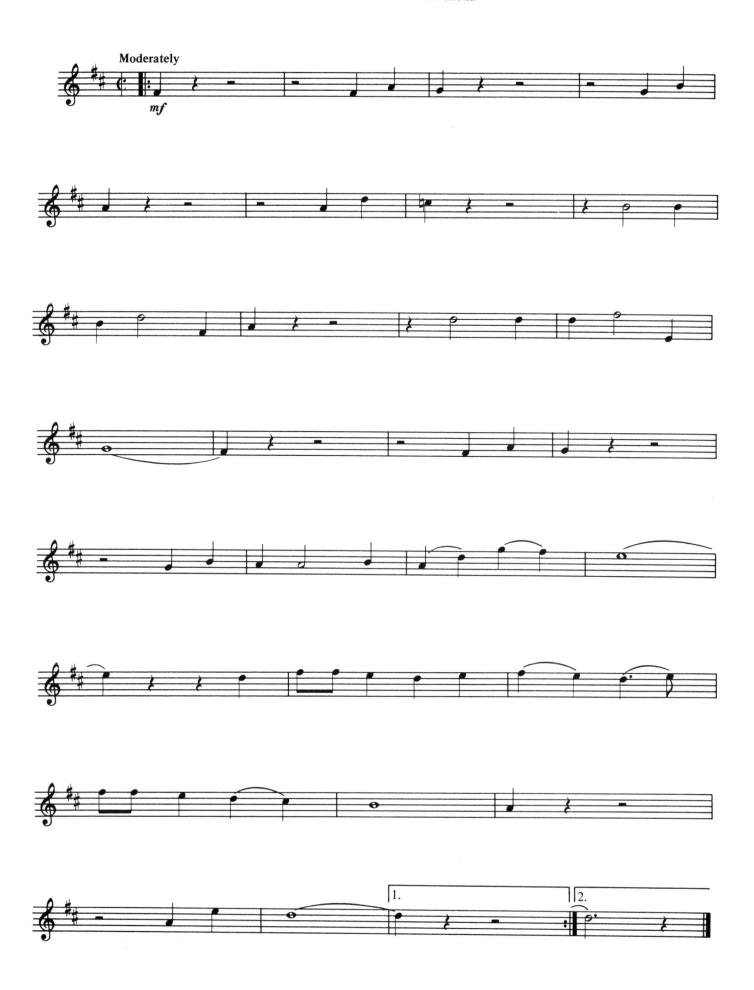

Where Have All The Flowers Gone.

Words and Music by Pete Seeger.

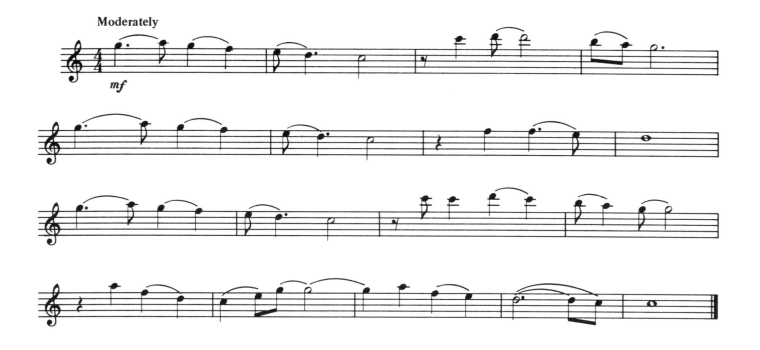

When The Saints Go Marching In.

Traditional.

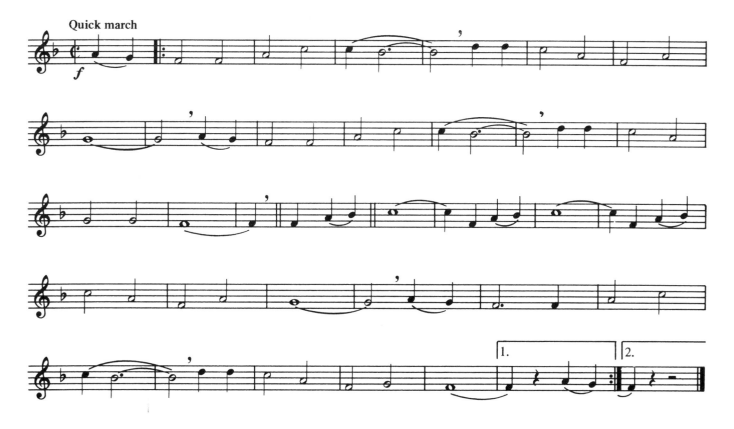

Kum Ba Yah.

Folk Song.

Love Me Tender.

Words and Music by Elvis Presley and Vera Matson.

A Dream Is A Wish Your Heart Makes.

Words and Music by Mack David, Al Hoffman and Jerry Livingston.

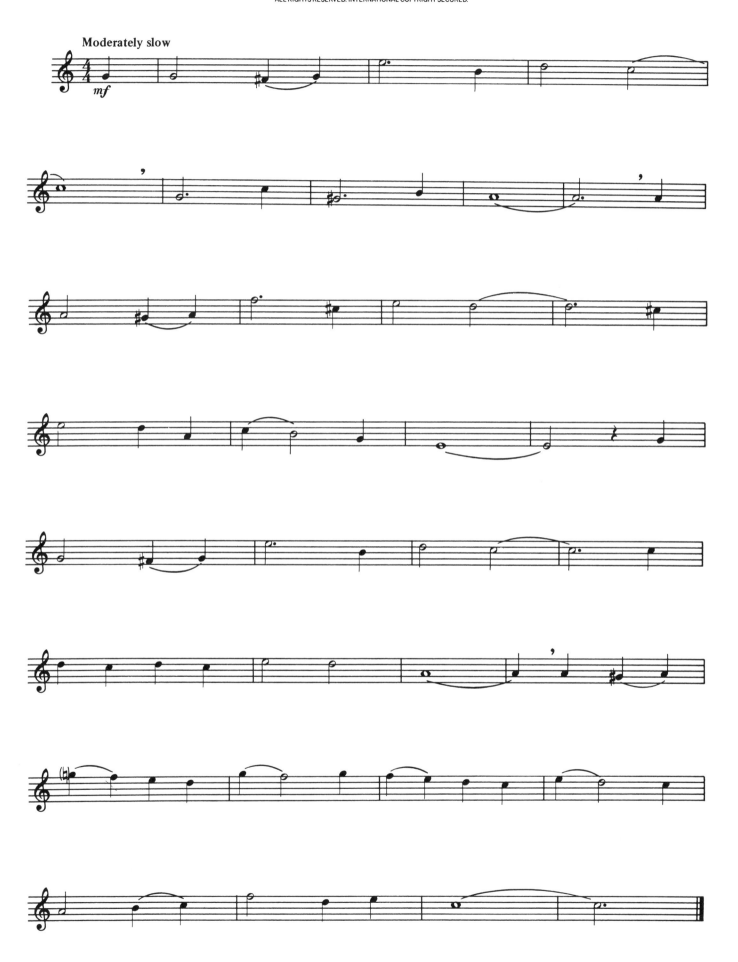

All My Loving.

Words and Music by John Lennon and Paul McCartney.

Knowing Me, Knowing You.

Words & Music by Benny Andersson, Stig Anderson & Bjorn Ulvaeus.

Moderately

Never Smile At A Crocodile.

Words by Jack Lawrence. Music by Frank Churchill.

As Long As He Needs Me.

Words and Music by Lionel Bart.

Moderato

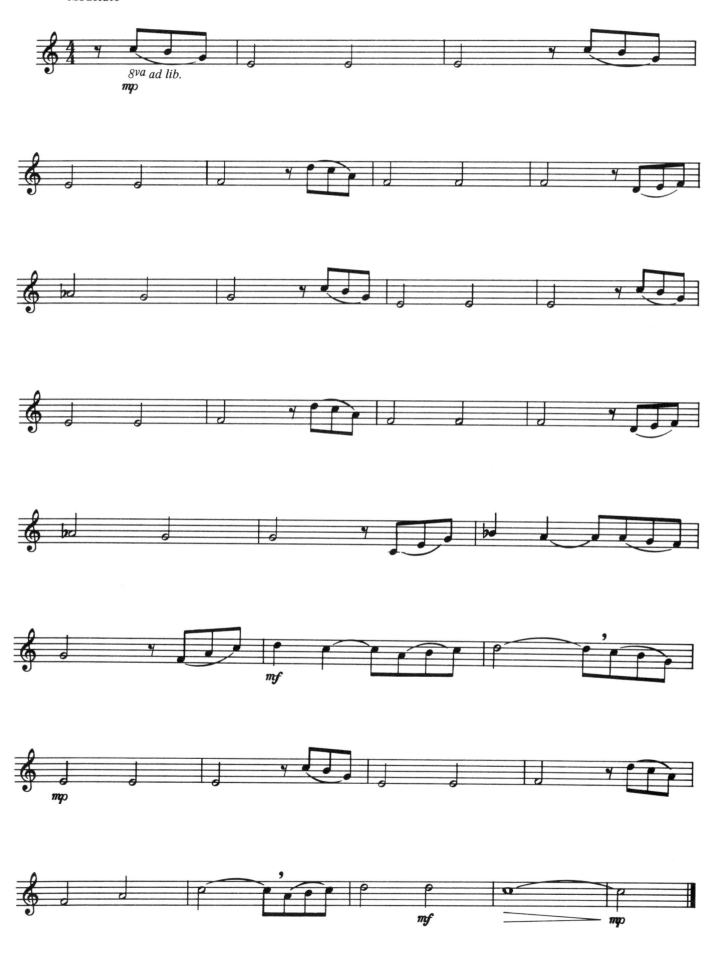

Norwegian Wood.
Words and Music by John Lennon and Paul McCartney.

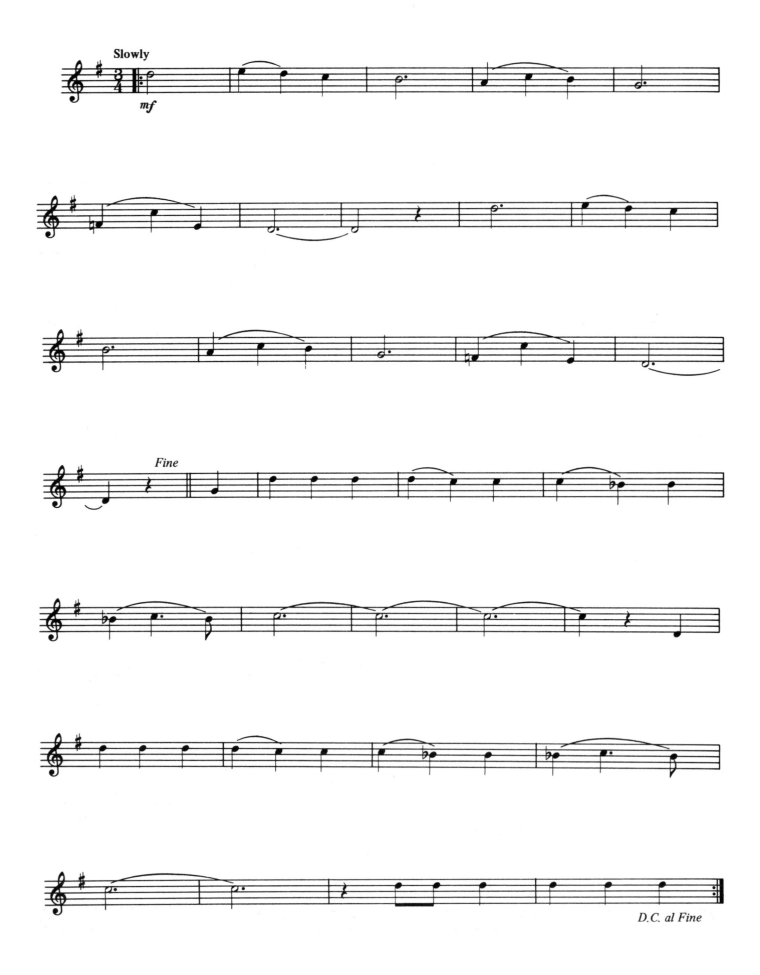

Pick A Pocket Or Two.
Words and Music by Lionel Bart.

Morning Has Broken.
Traditional.

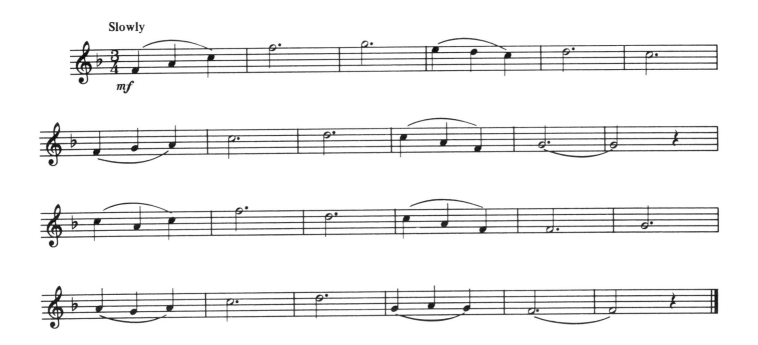

Scarborough Fair.

Traditional.

Moderately slow

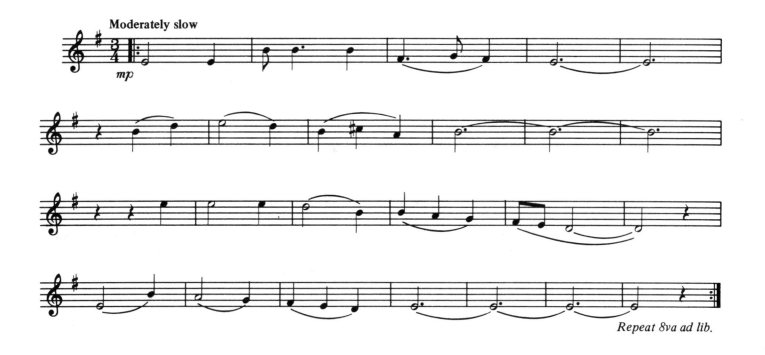

Repeat 8va ad lib.

Smile.

Words by John Turner and Geoffrey Parsons. Music by Charles Chaplin.

Andante

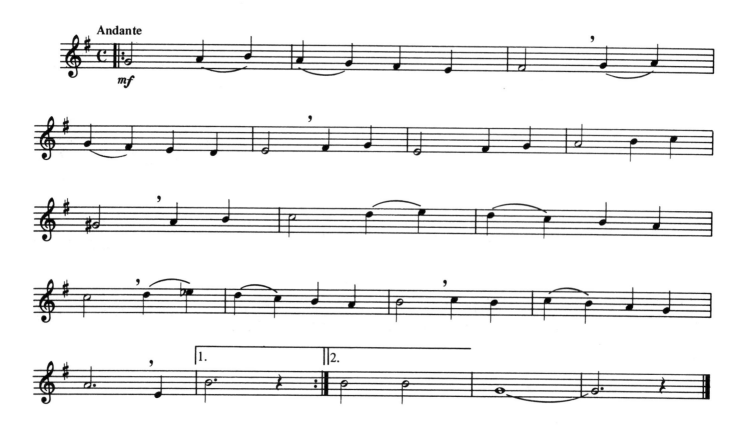

Bibbidi-Bobbidi-Boo

Words by Jerry Livingston. Music by Mack David and Al Hoffman.

Light Schottische Tempo

Country Gardens.
Traditional.

Moderato

Roses From The South.
By Johann Strauss, Jr.

Tempo di Valse

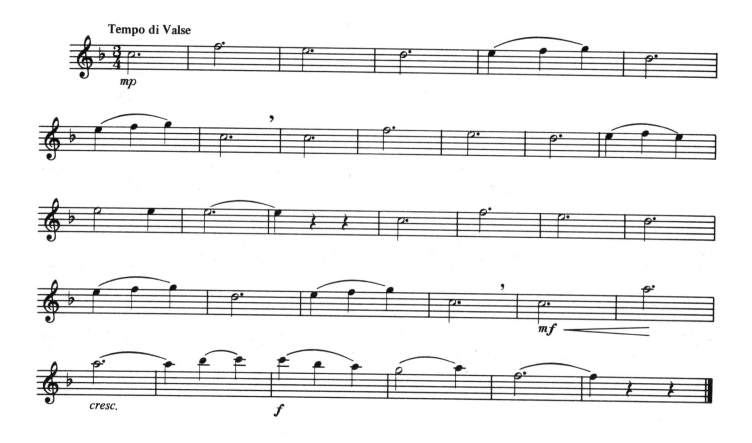

The Ballad of Davy Crockett.

Words by Tom Blackburn. Music by George Bruns.

Cielito Lindo.

Traditional

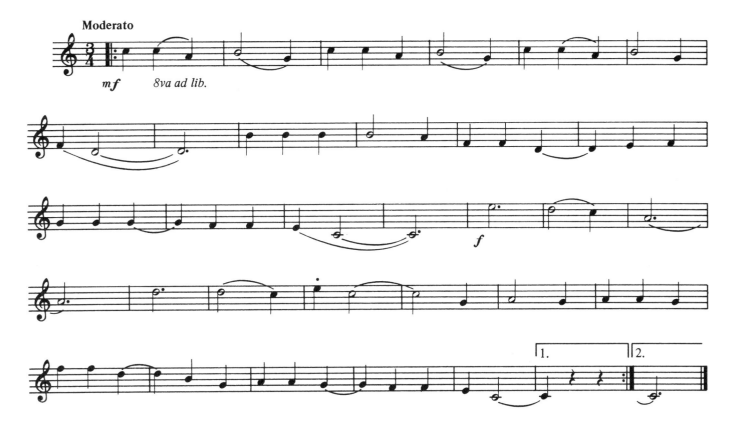

I'll Be Your Sweetheart.
Words and Music by Harry Dacre.

Moonglow.

Words and Music by Will Hudson, Eddie de Lange and Irving Mills.

Bring Me Sunshine.
Words by Sylvia Dee. Music by Arthur Kent.

With an easy swing

Sailing.
Words and Music by Gavin Sutherland.

21

Spanish Eyes.

Words by Charles Singleton and Eddie Snyder. Music by Bert Kaempfert.

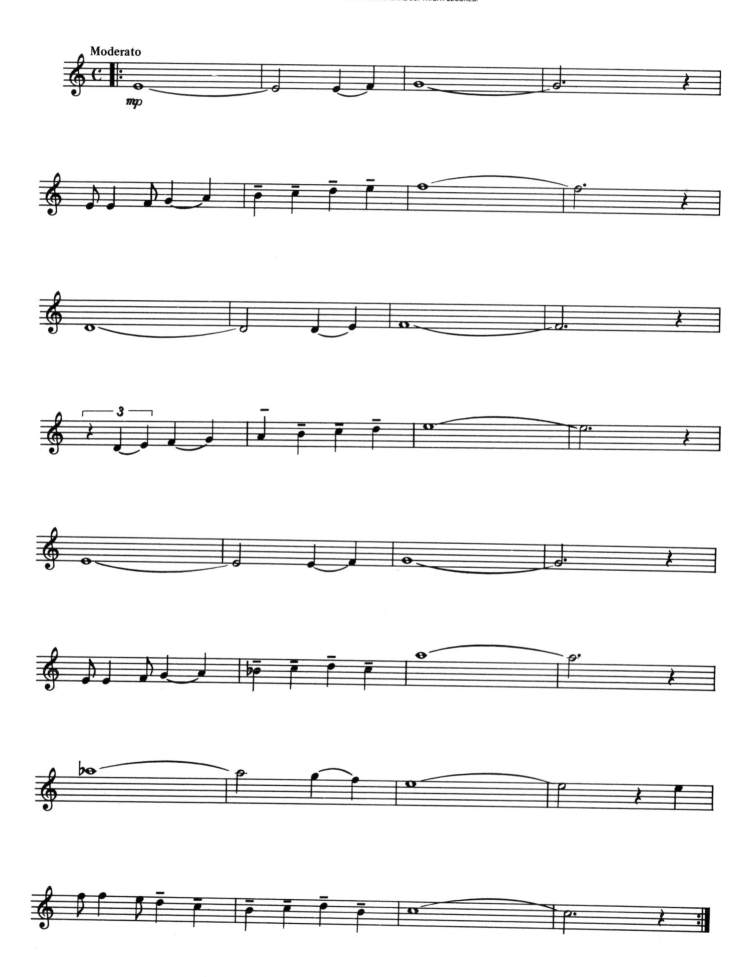

Streets Of London.
Words and Music by Ralph McTell.

A Spoonful Of Sugar.

Words and Music by Richard M. Sherman and Robert B. Sherman.

Brightly

After The Ball.

Words and Music by Charles K. Harris.

Moderately

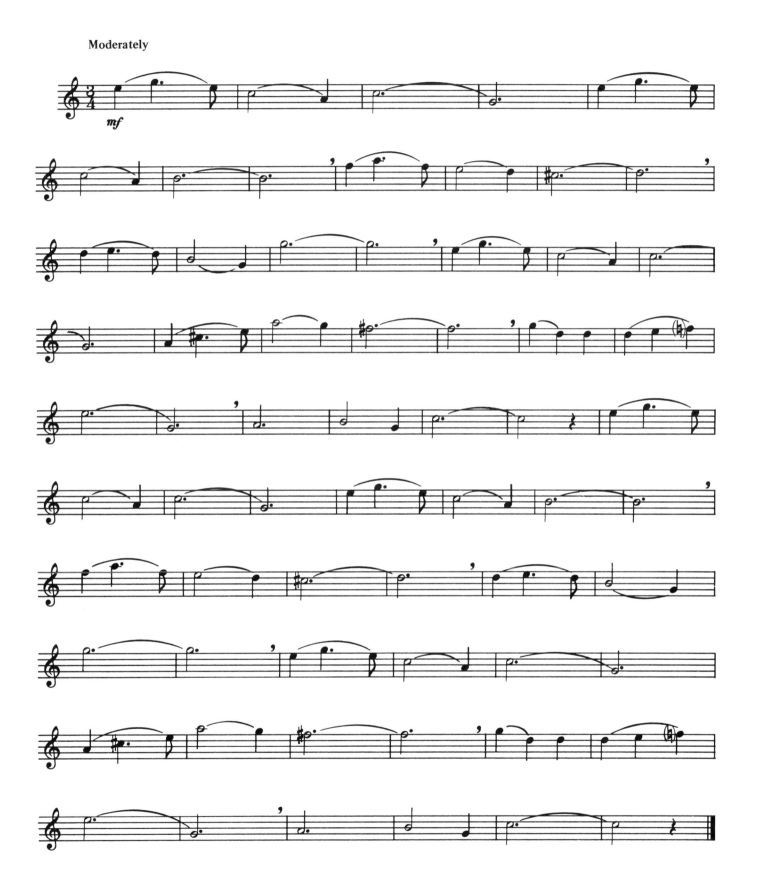

Wednesday's Child.
Words by Mack David. Music by John Barry.

Moderate waltz

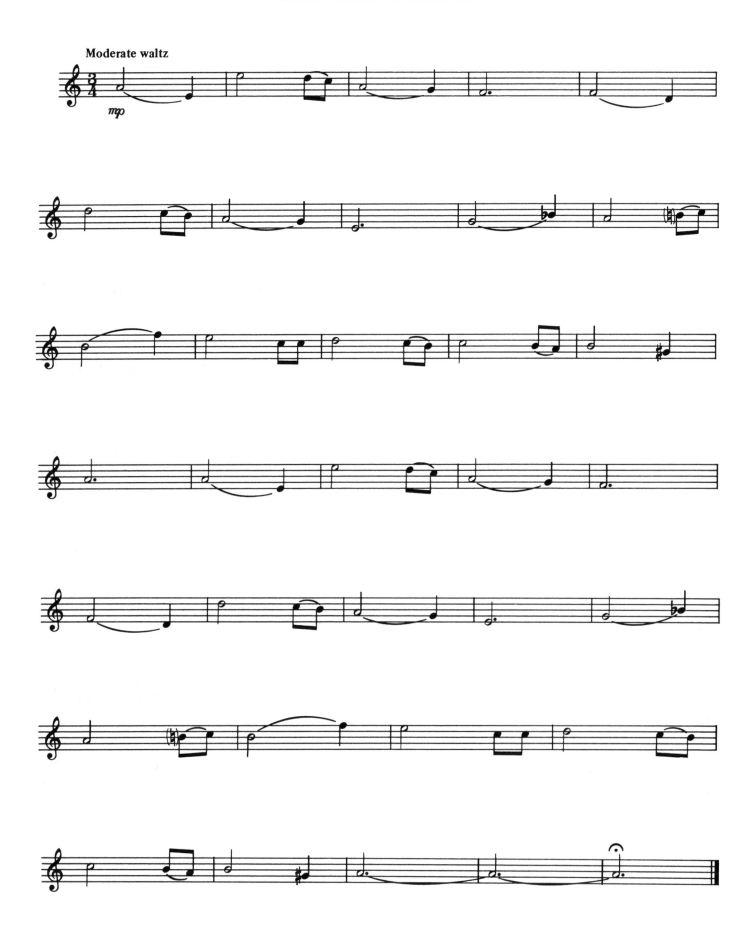

My Colouring Book.

Music by John Kander. Lyrics by Fred Ebb.

Gentle Waltz

Give A Little Whistle.
Words by Ned Washington. Music by Leigh Harline.

Strawberry Fields Forever.

Words and Music by John Lennon and Paul McCartney.

Steptoe And Son.

Music by Ron Grainer.

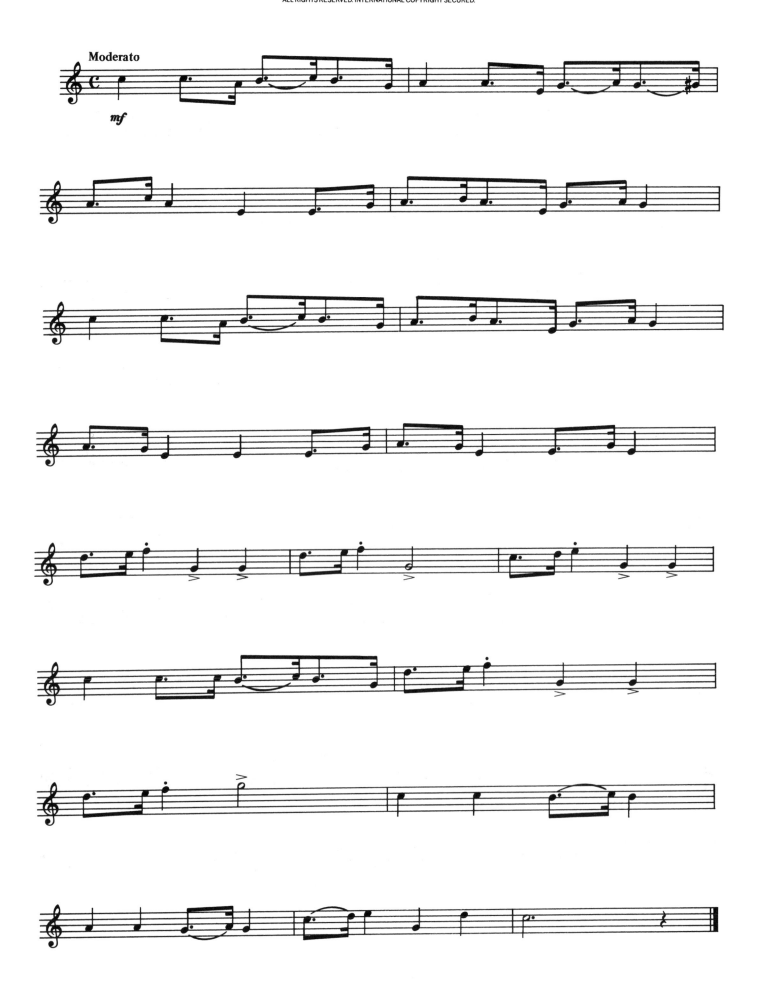

Please Don't Fall In Love.
Words and Music by Mike Batt.

She's Leaving Home.
Words and Music by John Lennon and Paul McCartney.

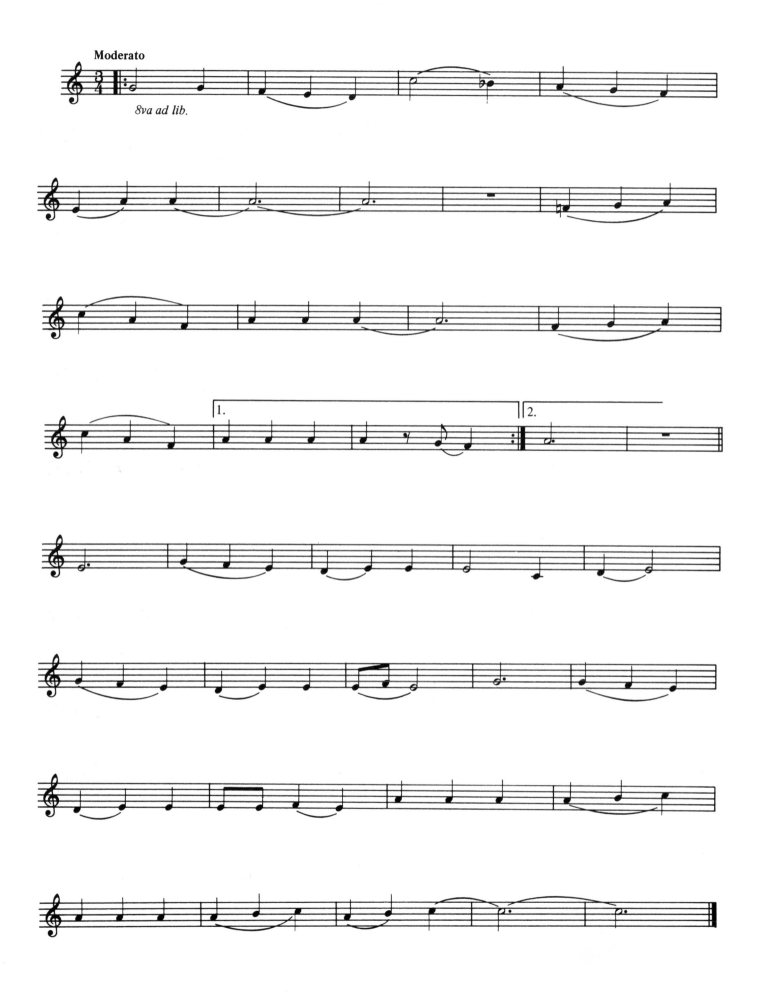

Never Never.

Words and Music by Vince Clarke.

Moderately

The Last Thing On My Mind.
Words and Music by Tom Paxton.

With feeling

Anniversary Song.
Words and Music by Al Jolson and Saul Chaplin.

Valse moderato

Don't Cry For Me Argentina.

Music by Andrew Lloyd Webber. Lyrics by Tim Rice.

Memories Are Made Of This.

Words and Music by Terry Gilkyson, Richard Dehr and Frank Miller.

Be Back Soon.

Words and Music by Lionel Bart.

Falling In Love Again.

Music and Original Words by Friedrich Hollander. English Words by Reg Connelly.

Waltz andante

Bright Eyes.
Words and Music by Mike Batt.

See You Later Alligator.
By Robert Guidry.

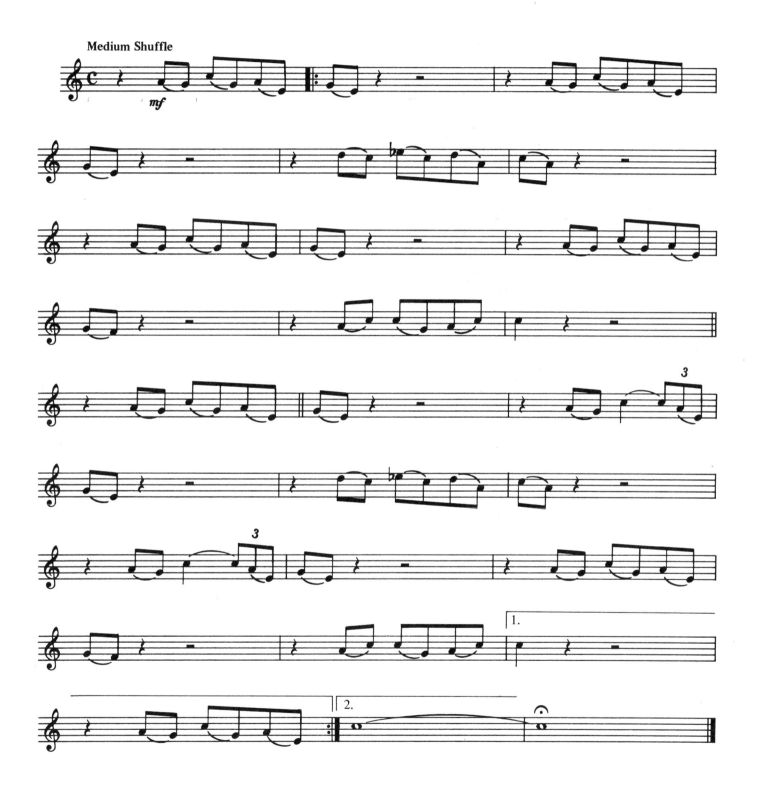

Fiddler On The Roof.

Music by Jerry Bock. Lyrics by Sheldon Harnick.

Moderato

How Can I Tell You.
Words and Music by Cat Stevens.

(Theme from) Crossroads.
By Tony Hatch.

Save Your Kisses For Me.

Words and Music by Tony Hiller, Lee Sheriden and Martin Lee.

Supercalifragilisticexpialidocious.

Words and Music by Richard M. Sherman and Robert B. Sherman.

On Wings Of Song.

By Felix Mendelssohn.

Who Do You Think You Are Kidding Mr Hitler?

Words by Jimmy Perry. Music by Jimmy Perry and Derek Taverner.

Move Over Darling.
Words and Music by Joe Lubin, Hal Kanter and Terry Melcher.

Fortuosity.

Words and Music by Richard M. Sherman and Robert B. Sherman.

Michelle.
Words and Music by John Lennon and Paul McCartney.

Honeysuckle Rose.

Music by Thomas 'Fats' Waller. Words by Andy Razaf.

Little April Shower.
Words by Larry Morey. Music by Frank Churchill.

Imagine.
Words & Music by John Lennon.

Moderately

When A Felon's Not Engaged In His Employment.

Words by W. S. Gilbert. Music by Arthur Sullivan.

Greensleeves.
Traditional.

Moderately

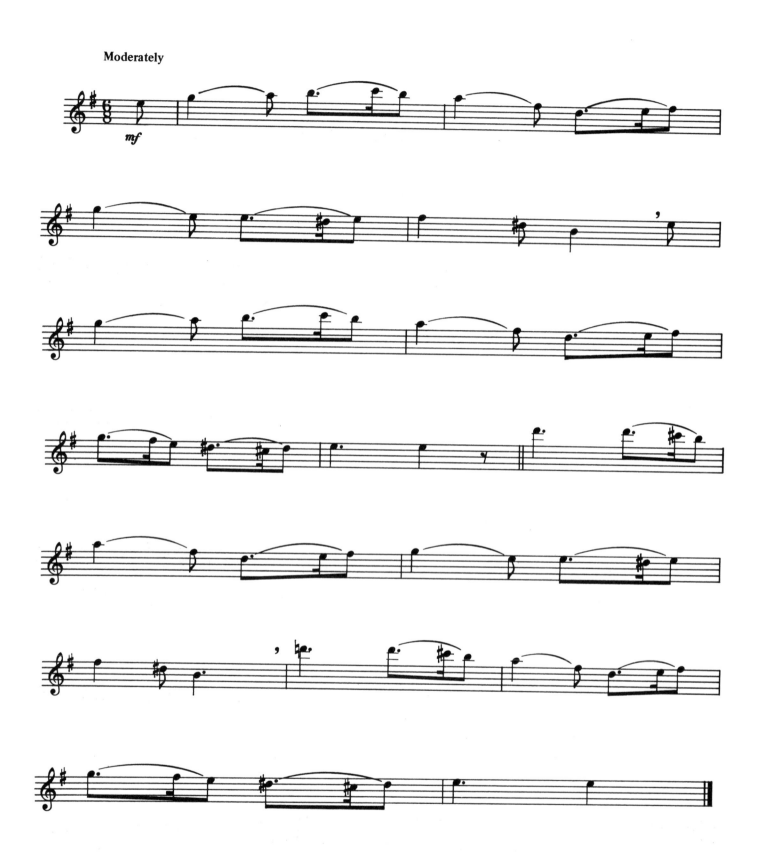

Swing Low, Sweet Chariot.
Traditional.

Serenade.
By Franz Schubert.

This Ole House.

Words & Music by Stuart Hamblen.

Moderately

Romance in G.
By Ludwig van Beethoven.

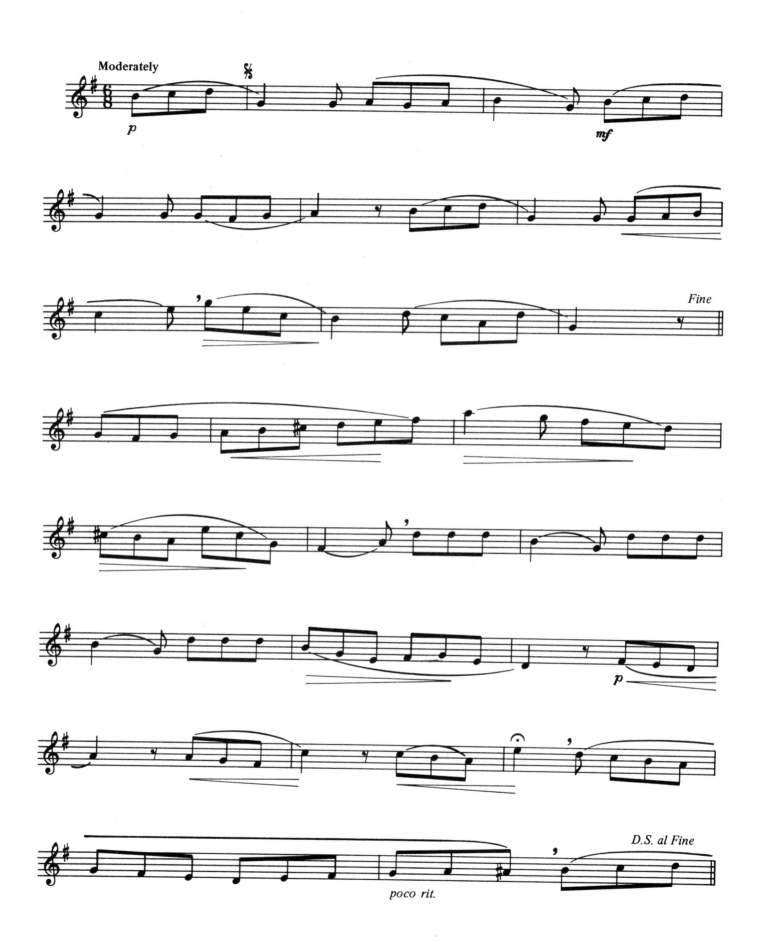

Where Is Love?

Words and Music by Lionel Bart.

When I'm Sixty-Four.
Words and Music by John Lennon and Paul McCartney.

Truly Scrumptious.
Words and Music by Richard M. Sherman and Robert B. Sherman.

Prelude in G Major.
By Frederik Chopin.

Prelude In D Minor.
By Frederik Chopin.

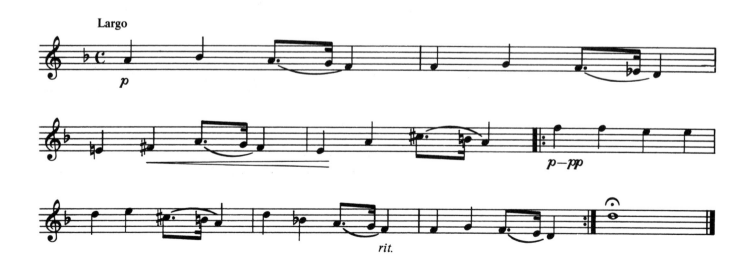

Who Will Buy?
Words and Music by Lionel Bart.

Chim Chim Cher-ee.
Words and Music by Richard M. Sherman and Robert B. Sherman.

Reviewing The Situation.
Words and Music by Lionel Bart.

I Don't Know How To Love Him.

Music by Andrew Lloyd Webber. Lyrics by Tim Rice.

Y Viva Espana.

English Words by Eddie Seago. Original Lyric by Leo Rozenstraeten. Music by Leo Caerts.

Little Boxes.
Words and Music by Malvina Reynolds.

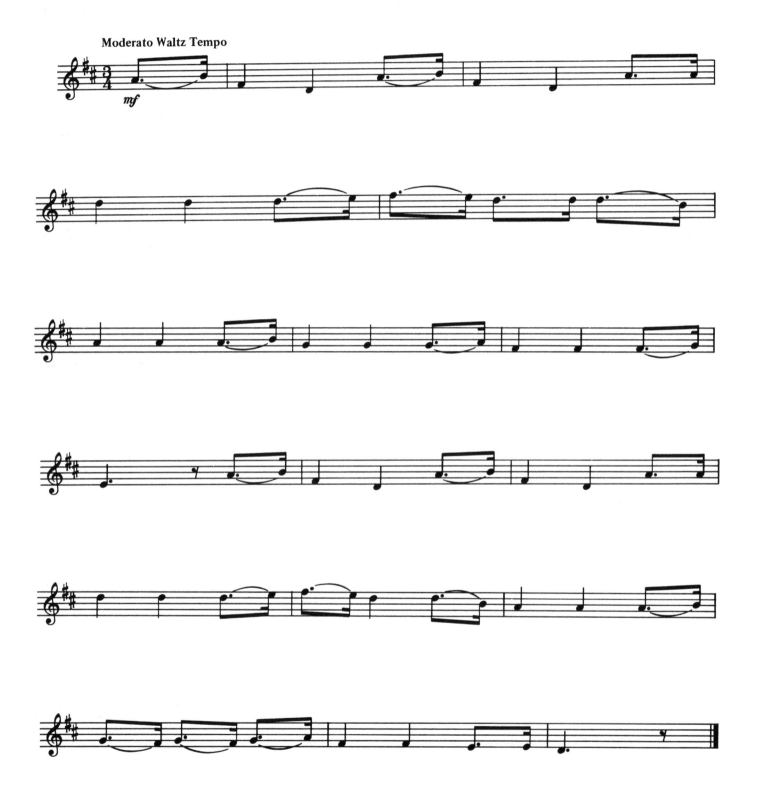

La Ci Darem La Mano (from 'Don Giovanni').
By Wolfgang Amadeus Mozart.

Nocturne.
By Alexander Borodin.

Food Glorious Food.

Words and Music by Lionel Bart.

Karma Chameleon.

Words and Music by O'Dowd, Moss, Hay, Craig and Pickett.

Ballade Pour Adeline.

Composer Paul de Senneville.

Moderately

poco rit.

I Think We're Alone Now.

Words & Music by Ritchie Cordell.

Moderately

Repeat and Fade

You Need Hands.
Words and Music by Max Bygraves.

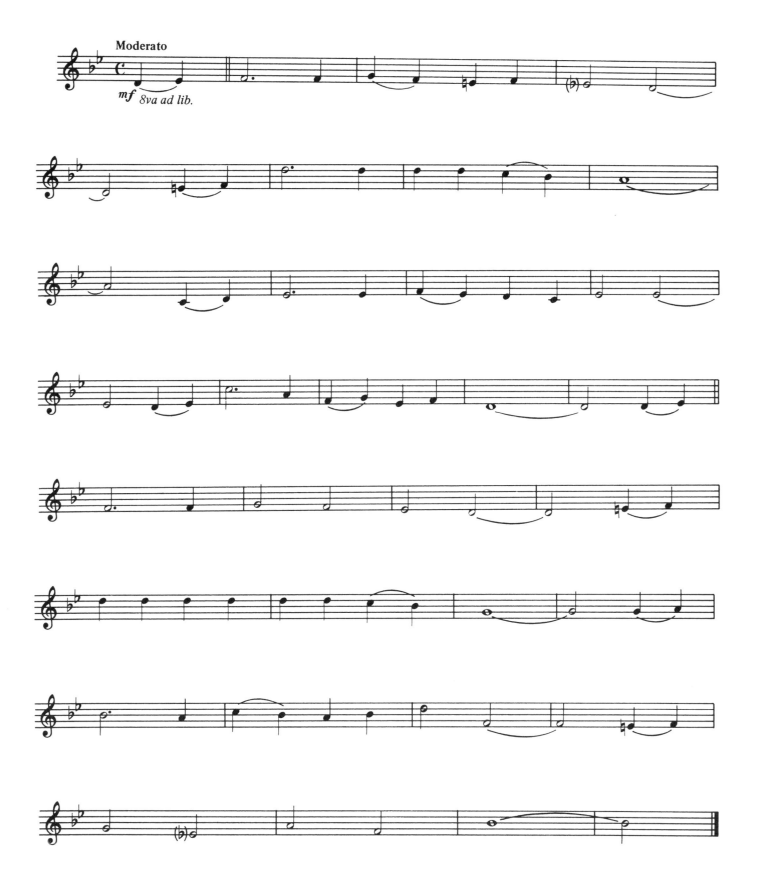

Oom Pah Pah.
Words and Music by Lionel Bart.

Yellow Submarine.

Words and Music by John Lennon and Paul McCartney.

Waterloo.
Words and Music by Benny Andersson, Stig Anderson and Bjorn Ulvaeus.

Swingin' Shepherd Blues.

Words by Rhoda Roberts and Kenny Jacobson. Music by Moe Koffman.

Consider Yourself.

Words and Music by Lionel Bart.

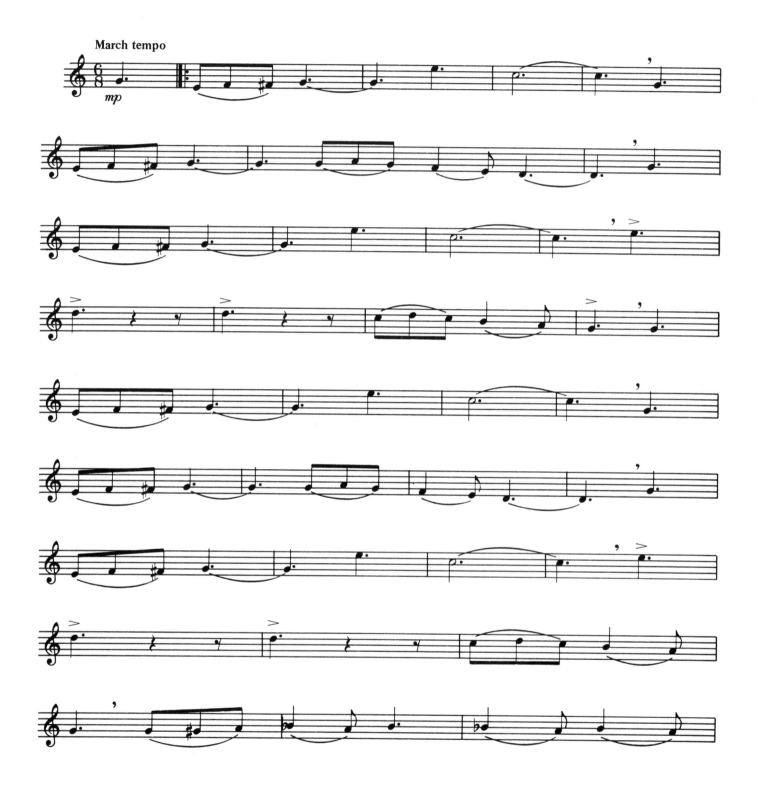

Yesterday Once More.
Words and Music by Richard Carpenter and John Bettis.

My Oh My.

Words and Music by N. Holder and J. Lea.

Moderately

poco rit.

Penny Lane.
Words and Music by John Lennon and Paul McCartney.

Lullaby of Birdland.
Music by George Shearing. Words by George David Weiss.

Carolina Moon.

Words by Benny Davis. Music by Joe Burke.

Basin Street Blues.

Words and Music by Spencer Williams.

Hawaii Five-O.
By Mort Stevens.

With a driving beat

Scottish Dance.

By Ludwig van Beethoven

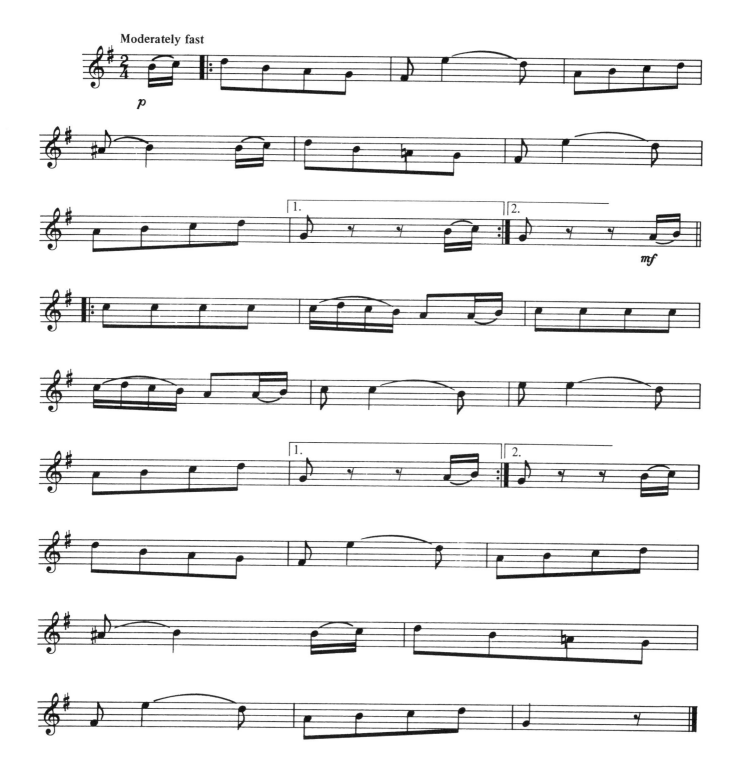

Radetzky March.

By Johann Strauss, Sr.

Underneath The Arches.
Words and Music by Bud Flanagan.

They Don't Know.
Words and Music by Kirsty McColl.

With A Little Help From My Friends.

Words and Music by John Lennon and Paul McCartney.

The Entertainer.
By Scott Joplin.

Printed in Great Britain by Redwood Books, Trowbridge, Wiltshire 10/96(26074)